a thirst

graham bowers

Such silence then before us, pinned against the wall,
Why need we whine? There is no way out, the birds
Will tell us nothing more; we shall vanish first,
Yet leave behind us certain frozen words
Which some day, though not certainly, may melt
And, for a moment or two, accentuate a thirst.

Louis MacNeice

© Graham Bowers 2017, 2019
First published 2017; 2nd edition 2019
All rights reserved

Published by BoD – Books on Demand, Stockholm, Sweden
Printed by BoD – Books on Demand, Norderstedt, Germany

ISBN: 9789176995860

Contents

Chronicle

a thirst

Canada Geese

As the morning haze thins
off the late-autumn field
the Canada Geese turn
and stretch towards the low sun.

And I understand their need:

Enter me, light and warmth!

From here

From this slope I've scrambled up
I see
all the others on their slopes,
the scree

loose and shifting
beneath us all
as we fight to keep our feet
against the pull.

There is no open vista
to admire,
the pull means that
we're constantly unsure

of how to climb,
why there's no level ground,
and who the others are
on either hand.

No point in waving or shouting:
we all know
for all our scrabbling
there's just one way to go;

the valley where we started out
at dawn
is where the pull will
force us to return.

Generally

More departures than destinations on all the journeys we make.
We learn a bit, we don't-learn a lot, and are constantly forced to resort
to ad hoc navigation along routes we never sought,
paying for every wrong turn, and no clear charts to be bought.

We try to keep ourselves together, but we flake –
though this can help us take on board things we never thought
would be added to our baggage on these journeys that we make.

We like the idea of a meaning, but it's one we must forsake.
We try to keep on an evenish keel, but our keel keeps getting caught,
and the only feeling we really know is of generally falling short
on the stop-start, hit-miss, forward-backward journeys that we make.

Wishful thinking

Imagine if you could
round the corner
square all the angles
triangulate your position cleanly.

Co-ordinates under control,
no tangents to be spun off at,
able to stay
true to your origin,
unbisected, centred.

Girl on Bike

The little girl on her bike
goes round and round the yard between the houses,
round and round
for pure joy of being
able to do it,
in that way where, when you've mastered something
it happens through and with you
as much as you do it.

No destination or route plan
but pure bike-riding,
like a bird that has just learnt to fly
and is brim-full of the need
to swoop and zip.

Rapt in commitment, focus, balance,
as if she will be able to do this,
go on fizzing through the total present,
for as long as she likes:
not just till tea-time
but in an undemanding, time-free forever.

A Flurry

Snow – a long-term temporary thing,
grabs all the attention while it's here.
Comes late autumn, stays into spring,
so dominant you forget it's a temporary thing
till it's gone and the blanketless life can begin.
The hardness of the rock beneath can reappear
when snow's time's up – it's a temporary thing,
though it grabbed all the attention while it was here.

Work

The things that I may say to you
have, of course, no special weight.
I do not catch and chain the truth,
I would not claim to channel light.
It's like when rocks in fields in spring
ache themselves from underground
up into view. Like landscaping:
you drag and shift the things you find,
you drain and roll, hedge and stumble.
And everything being resonant
with undertow and parable,
this simply aims to document
how in the things we do perhaps we're all
just trying to gain a grip on stone and soil.

The One Song

If I could draw
I'd sketch your face, your form,
and nothing else, again and again.

If I could sing
I'd sing just the one song,
of your hardly-awake morning smile
when I bring you coffee in bed.

If I could build
I'd be Isambard Kingdom Bowers
and construct a fantastic feat of a bridge,
a span of praise
across which I travel to you every day.

Phnom Kulen

Researchers using delicately calibrated
light-pulsing scanners from the air have found
old cities, canals, temples, all highly
developed and sophisticated,
swallowed by centuries of jungle
under the Cambodian ground.

Which goes to show:

All mankind's best efforts to extend
the boundaries, create and solve – the fruits
of our endeavours being demonstrations
not to higher powers but to ourselves –
when the soil subsumes them in the end
they are not lost but feed the future's roots.

All mankind's best efforts to achieve
and impose order, the systems that get built,
all we do to be the best and prove it –
and likewise everything each one of us
does and makes and thinks and might believe –
in time it founders and is lost in silt.

Home and Away

All those great migrators –
swifts, martins,
salmon, eels –
because this is where we are
we talk about them coming home.

But equally, the place they come from
(or go back to)
viewed from there
is home.

Though, come to think of it,
most of their time they're on the move,
so perhaps it's more accurate to say
migration is their home.

Is that the way to do it?

Museum

I am a museum.
And I'm the curator.
Or, one of the curators is me.
The other ones are me as well
(or at least they used to be).

For all the generous opening hours
and my no-charge policy,
for those who enter there are galleries
and repositories I can't unlock,
not having been entrusted with the key.

Those pictures they can view
(which I sometimes think
I curate coherently),
and the fossils and displays and empty spaces,
they interpret independently

of whatever the labels I provide might say.
Then, via the hall of mirrors,
they leave, lost in thought or thought-free.
I pick up things they've dropped
and add them to the installation called "Temporary/

Permanent: what's left", and then
I close any windows opened inadvertently
and go wherever curators go, leaving
the museum to its nocturnal devices
(there's only low-level security).

"Clarity", he said

"Clarity", he said,
"that's what I want.
Cut out all the loose-skeined stuff
that clogs and obscures.
Get things straight and tight –
you know: one and one is two.
Scrape it all down to simplicity,
only the absolutes left."

"Fine", she said,
"but I have a feeling
the absolutes are far from simple.
And anyway:
what do you mean by clarity?
What are you actually going to do?
And what principle ensures
the simple and the absolute
(whatever they are) per se are always right?

"That 'loose-skeined stuff' – that's what life is.
The threads don't weave neatly together.
There are sags and snags, rough patches and flaws.
Things happen, our control is pretty slight,
we can't get all our edges plumb-line true.

"I'm sorry if this sounds smart-arse enigmatic
or epigrammatic,
but clarity for me means being able
to accept the lack of clarity.
Our own life is not something we can view
from a perspective-giving height,
and simplicity means taking what comes,
filtering out while acknowledging
the filter lets everything through.

"So darling, sure, we can paint the walls white,
but the brickwork's still there,
it's just out of sight."

Preparation

He screwed down the weather-vane
to define all winds as being from the south,
bearers of warm summer evenings, or
the lapwings returning
ready for the spring.

He stopped the clock at seven.
7 am – a fresh start,
the day clean and open.
7 pm – a sheaf of possibilities
ready to untie themselves.

He never locked the door,
so all visitors could step straight into the kitchen
where he always cooked enough for several,
with extra plates and cutlery
ready on attentive stand-by.

But no-one knocked.

And of course the wind blew
the winter in from the north and east,
blew wild and wet from the west.

And he was never in time
for any of the trains he could have caught.

Urban Nature

"I'm not in charge of sorrow"
goes the song in my ears
as I walk through the park.

And a squirrel
darts across the path
and starts up a tree.

Quick russet movements
warm and alive.
I halt and it stops,
flits behind the trunk,
then reappears, poising
its perfect balance along a branch.

In this town though not of it,
fading all the noise to background haze.
Nearly touching distance
as we focus each other.

Then it flickers
up and out of sight.
Warm and lithe,
here and gone, in and out,
like you.

And the sorrow takes charge.

Sycamore

The sycamore will wedge and nudge
in anywhere there's a gap, or hint
of a gap,
then grow and spread to fill the space.

Early seeder, the clustered pods
muster like parachutists, ready
for the drop,
to make the future now, all sensors braced.

Needing and asking no favours,
the survivor that takes over,
quick to tap
into whatever rations it can take.

More twig and scrag than well-wrought bough.
No time for slow and solid grace, no doubt.
Resilience of aim, of limbs that
do not snap.

Whippy, lusty, no false modesty.
The broad leaves hog the light, their veins
like a map
of how to win, how to push up and out.

The Cenotaph

The emblematic
structure, the casing
the traffic passes by.

I wonder where I'm really buried.

Distance

She was always looking
for the apposite act,
the germane gesture.

At a remove,
unwilling to identify with
the unwieldy commerce of just
living and doing, getting by.

So instead of staying
(shorthand for fighting
                doubting
                resigning
                eroding
                facing,
                not going)
she gave me
a rose for the garden
that would never die,
and left.

Stéphane and Django

Grappelli

The way the notes
pour themselves into
and out of each other,
like wild-thyme-and-orange honey.

Not even needing to coax them
as they roll and bloom and
layer themselves over any sharp edges,

as though he accepts
that the notes come to him, through him,
and spreads that acceptance to us.

Reinhardt

The way the notes
punch themselves into
life, open and affirmative.

Setting them up and letting them go,
coaxing them, fretting them,
welcoming
their edginess

as though, defiant in his understanding
that all does not go well
unless we are ready to make it,
he spreads that defiance to us.

Grappelli and Reinhardt

The way the music
defines itself,
driving and soothing
in its spread and gather,

their mastery giving us
a sense that we too might be able
to get things into shape, under control,
uniting the threads,
defiant and accepting,
creating a whole.

As though we can make their antiphony ours –
the warp and the weft,
the bird and the nest;
you be the bed
and I'll be the flowers.

I'll be the rhythm that sets free your tune
You be the glass and I'll pour the wine
We'll both be the darkness
We'll both be the moon.

Skin

Your skin your skin
I can't begin
to swim
against the tide
released by your hide
as you roll against my side.

The sweet warm line
of your hips and behind
you turn and align
your lips on mine
and press your chest
against my chest.

Surely you never
need to get dressed?

Types

When he enters any gathering
his self-assurance is
like a big four-stroke motorbike,
cruiser handlebars and all,
which he rides smoothly into the room,
bom, bom, bom.
No helmet, of course –
hair combed back, easy smile,
ready to feel at home and in control.

‡

She lifted down the moon
and polished it gently in her long, soft hair,
hung it round and warm
where I could always see it
in the corner of my window,
and went south for the winter.

‡

His talk was a collection of punchlines
that had never been near a joke.
Planned, pre-scripted, straining
to be amusing or pithy –
achieving neither, unengaging:
the ultimate unfunny bloke.

‡

A town of unspectacularly unlovely
buildings,
streets, blocks, districts, all
embodiments of function, and function alone.
No thought of soothing the eye, or
picturesquing the townscape.
No scope for escapes
on this or any other wet, grey morning.
Why provide visitors
with postcardly vistas
when there are jobs to be done,
needs to be met,
lives to be led.

‡

He was always saying things like
"If I'd thought I'd ever get
what I was waiting for,
I'd have stopped waiting
as soon as I started" –

things which he thought sounded like
he'd reached a level of insight
beyond the rest of us, things like

"The important thing in life
is to have no regrets,
since that shows your life is like an arrow
flying truly towards your fuller self."

Sententious prick.

‡

A magpie
with its light, tight, sparky bounce
along a ledge halfway up a building,
left and right,
round the corner and back again.
Astute, attuned, assessing
when to peck and pick,
nip in and snap up –
ready for every off-chance
and on-chance.

‡

"Good idea",
he'd say,
"but who will bell the cat?"
Or
"Time and tide wait for no man,
so best strike while the iron's hot."

Always a ready adage
he could stand behind, like a safety rope,
reminding the world fortune favours the brave,
looking before urging others to leap.

‡

Ask her and she always answers
"You know, between jobs", or
"Well, you know, ready to move on",
with a deflecting, not very convincing smile.

Ask her and she always says
"You know, between men", or
"Well, you know, ready to move on",
with a not very convincing
but clearly enquiry-ending smile.

Ducks the radars,
so who's to know:
unfulfilled,
lacking the weight to take root –
or in her natural habitat,
good at being
between jobs, between men,
able to meet life,
although it's not very convincing,
with a smile.

Parallel

We're parallel, I'm sorry
for all that that entails.
Stretching out together, side by side,
but for however far, between the rails
there will always be divide.

Into forever always closeness,
we know there can be no track
with one but not the other.
Yet heading forwards in next-to-ness
there's the same close distance if we look back.

A Word

Hyleg.
Not being learned or superstitious
I didn't know the word before,
dressed trimly in dictionary Arial,
it surfaced into view
in the lower focal field of my glasses
when I was looking for something else.

"The ruling planet at the hour of birth."

Some words are like origami-folded
layers and shapes
that open themselves outwards leaf by flap,
or those maze-like ideograms
that suck you in towards their centre,
and get you thinking
about life,
yourself,
your life.

Heaney Suite
(Seamus Heaney, 1939–2013)

(i) Gårdlösa Stones

Summer segueing into autumn when he died.
The landscape/manscape here is Tollund-like
and I walked down, over the stile, along the stream,
and up through the trees to the stone ship on its rise.

Unfussed-over: old, not grand – just a few
rough stones left now on their holm, a fact
among the other farmland facts. A scent-mark – marking what?
Burial? Standing? A boundary view?

Up the lane, red kite circling with their time-slowing swing,
to where the iron-age girl was found in the moss
with a silver brooch. A sacrifice? No – no noose
was found, no hanging-cap, no cut-throat gape

(though the stranglers and slitters are on the move here too,
hunting voodoo victims for their blunt bone spikes:
all parishes have man-killing in them at closer sight).
More stone circles here, anchored in earth

tilled over centuries but now at sea
in flats of too-clean maize and stem-stunted wheat:
no headrigs, plough-socks, or patience of hooves and feet.
And embedded in the wind that threads through stands of oak
and beech, the whine of traffic.

Boundary crossing
is all we do, though no cairns mark the lines we cross.
I am at home here, by which I mean
as not-at-home as anywhere else. As he said:
not at odds or at one, but simply lost.

(ii) Wintering in

Wintering in
Hunkering down
Tightening up.

Shoulders hunch to meet the strain.
Horizons contract.
Not much to see, the outlook known.

Cutting back
Digging in
Digging deep.

Branches rid themselves of green,
supply lines are cut to the delicate
stuff that would distract or drain.

Staying taut
Shoring up
Squaring off.

Sole focus on joining the dots
of the thin line
from solstice to equinox.

(iii) Dialect

The Durham holidays were an ear-opener.
Dialect like the stone farmhouse:
unflinchingly local,
standing its ground.

A language within the language,
each variant vowel a declaration of independence,
our cousins' "go" nearly rhyming with "paw".
We had croggies on bikes,
and cobbing a clemmie was something other
than throwing a stone
(as sallies and whins were what Heaney saw).

A tongue rooted in the loam
of particular earth – in the swim of itself
in the unassuming, unapologetic way
of the beer-brown Tees, or the Moyola.
Like a pre-global music, on the human scale
and thus valid beyond its own borders,
as the farmhouse windows framed,
when looking out, a different landscape
in the same country.

What is true (the centring weight)

The truth, or sense
of truth, is not the facts.
And it's not about what is at stake:
it's the authentic centring weight
in circumstance, in words, in acts,
that is not made, but self-locates.

It is not left, it is not right,
it is not day, it is not night.
It's not the dove, it's not the crow,
it's not above, it's not below.
It does not whisper, does not roar –
it's just what is, it's just the core.

It is not can or must or ought,
it can't be sold, can't be bought.
It is not night, it is not day,
it's not the goal, it's not the way.
It's not of chains or being free,
it's not of you, far less of me.

It's not the dove, not the crow,
it's not composed of yes or no.
Don't think in terms of less or more –
it's just what is, it is the core.

Within what's done, within what's said,
it goes beyond just heart, just head,
it goes beyond being safe and sound,
it's straight and narrow, broad and round.
It is not win or loss or draw –
it's just what is, it is the core.

Don't talk effect, do not talk cause,
don't look for medals or applause.
It's sometimes silk and sometimes stone,
sometimes blood and sometimes bone.
It isn't random, isn't fate,
it is both weight and counterweight.

It needs no sparkle, needs no spin,
it is not virtue, is not sin.
It's not what we believe or hope,
it is not meme, it is not trope.
It's not what if, it's not what for –
it's just what is, it's just the core.

It's not of hurt, it's more than love,
it's not the crow, it's not the dove.
It is not hers, it is not his –
it's just the core, it's just what is.

Johan and Leonard

Cruyff and Cohen,
two masters who have gone
behind the curtain, gone down the tunnel.

Great capnomancers in their day;
cowled in smoke, through whose ribboning scrolls
clear vision was borne in to them,
them being of the seeing kind.

The defiant footballer,
philosopher and social questioner
(so pale and skinny when younger
it looked like smoke
was not only what he breathed,
but all he ate),
whose thinking moved between the lines,
opened the angles
and made space out wide.

The dense and weightless wavelengths
where the man of words found
words and notes of balanced weight.
The voice deepened,
the sounding line deepened
by a life of exposure to the unfiltered truth.
Emotional quester
whose thoughts moved on and between the lines
and brought space into the centre.

Total commitment to getting it right.
Formulators, encompassers,
direction-givers.

Johan Cruyff: 1947–2016
Leonard Cohen: 1934–2016

Her Song

I am his anchor in the tides of time,
I centre his circle, date-line his map.
You can count the years but not bound the time

because the cord that does not snap
is rooted and linked outside of time,
it unbars the cage, unwires the trap

and compasses the pulse of time
– so clock-bound swift yet slow as stone.
Our lungs, as much as air, breathe time,

and it sediments within our bone –
I feel its weight from all the time
my heart absorbed, time that was thrown

onto the wind, time that has blown
through my veins; and yet I've known
that what enfolds us won't unwrap:
though stretched and tested, like sails that flap
but do not fail, it brought him home
to me, to love, in time.

The Modern World – a Villanelle

There are things such as need to be brought home;
we know them but prefer to dodge the truth:
mankind can never live by growth alone.

Commerce per se need not be overthrown:
be it bacon, or tiles to mend the roof,
there are such things as need to be brought home.

But these are not the reason we were born.
Famine and global warming are the proof
mankind should not believe in growth alone.

Attention smothered by the frothing foam,
within the mass we're atoms on the hoof,
lost in a sightless undergrowth, alone.

The deserts, wars and poison show we're torn.
Vested interests lead, we follow suit,
yet yearn for a truer compass to bring us home

to a place where love and peace can set the tone,
and life unfold, a stem with real roots.
We know it, but it needs to be brought home:
mankind can never live by growth alone.

I Give

I give to you
my wish to be
engulfed by you
limitlessly.

I give the depths
to which I fall,
my needing heart
with its begging bowl.

I give (a giving
beyond choice)
my wild desire
my quietest voice,

my unsure strength,
my wish to live.
Take this, love:
the love I give.

"My heart the shape of a begging bowl" ~ Leonard Cohen, "Undertow"

Reading history books,

it can seem that in the distant past, to live was to express
belonging and commitment, the centralities of life.
The people were rooted, unequivocal, not at odds with time.
When working or resting, or making figurines;
their songs, their food, their clothes: none of it disconnected
surfaces; it all bound them to their humanity, their earth.

Was everything true and taut, charged and connected?
Not as a matter of style – they were anchored in their life.
Could, then, seeking daily totems help me find the core in mine?
When eating, I'll feel how plate, knife and fork are expressions
of how we've learned to harness what is given by the earth,
how brain and hands have freed us from being penned in by our genes.

And food not just refuelling, but an act of reconnection
with the self-renewing meaning of sun and air and earth,
a bond that's sealed with water, or the alchemy of wine.
And dressing, undressing, washing, sleeping, will not just be routines
but heedful acts, a gathered breath, to reset the expression
of being engaged, directed, a life that is in and of life.

And can I find, in our age, work to help me feel earthed,
so the current that runs through me is the human pulse that means
I'm meshed, not in transactions but in actions that align
me with some undeflected inner and outer truth, a life
that is not submerged in products, since what they express
is a counting down of hours, overridden, unconnected.

Of course they too were getting through the day, not expressly
embodying a blessed state for us to read as a still life;
they were living, in motion and emotion, not enacting memes
of balance and belief, of congruence with their earth.
But back-lit by them our sense of being adrift is underlined:
we're out of kilter, footing gone, where they seem so connected.

Implications

Implications
always go beyond
actual acts,
the narrative facts
of given situations.

The stone gives one splash,
then sinks, is gone.
But the rings pulse and widen
like self-
propagating suggestions.

What does it mean?
is a question that
cannot be compassed,
as echoes, whispers,
cross-currents,
spread in so many
directions.

Split

She yinned my yang
to hell
and not back.
We exchanged more cross words
than you get in a month of Sunday
papers.

We split along our fault lines
and now, left here
like a catapult with no elastic,
in rooms still recovering,

there's no respite
from her goneness.

Heron

Do I like the heron because
it shows me things I wish
it was in me to be?
Of course it's noble –
all animals are noble,
because being noble
means being true.

Because, in its unfussy focus,
standing in the water or returning to its tree,
it is at one
with what it is and what it does?
Of course it is –
all animals are at one.

Doing its best – without trying –
to look like a no-unnecessary-extras
Japanese drawing,
it is heron
wordlessly,
no sign of even noticing
the train I pass in behind it.

Clearance

I've been trying to give myself a wide berth,
not thinking "what would I do, what's in line with me?",
sidelining the idea of me as a touchstone for things' worth.

You get up in the morning and what needs to be
done, or what can be done, asks you if you will or won't
do it, but doesn't ask you to pronounce on being free.

Things concatenate and cross-weave, or they don't,
there are gaps and jumps and sideward steps,
missing stitches, some things lost, others spent.

Life, identity – it's not a kit that snaps
neatly together and coheres as if it's glued;
neither self nor world is static, pieces break, fabric rips.

What we are and what confronts us inform what we do,
and as we act, in part our deeds do us into being
what we are, what we become and what we will go through.

Though this does not annul the idea of meaning.
It's not a declaration saying "I don't care
what I do or what it leads to." Values, fellow-feeling

are in our lode. This is no call for laissez-faire.
Nor is it abdication. In fact it's a strict régime:
"personality" is no excuse, with all the masks we wear.
Whatever I do I've no-one, not even my self, to blame.

Iconoclasms

(i) Haiku

Paper kimono.
I don the holy robe with
seventeen stitches.

Dawn's brush inks the trees
on the washi of the day.
Joe the cat stretches.

I invest myself
with balanced breath, elliptic eye:
roshi, yogi, sage.

I fold my verbs flat.
Enigmatic, restrained. Now
kensho can emerge.

Seventeen – no more
or less. Not eight. Not forty.
Something in me cries:

Emperor, you're cold:
Get free, get moving, get dressed!
There's no reason why

truth can only be
three lines, of five/seven/five.
Clipped wings do not fly.

(ii) Lund Cathedral

Towers and pyramid roofs lift skywards,
every massive block minutely square and true,
the masonry impeccable – rounded arches, colonettes, the works.

And I've been to Salisbury, too,
and Reims. And heritage or not, they chafe and offend,
all these monuments, not to a greater glory

but to the great and few, with their imaginary friend
and very real earthly power with its age-old foundation
of self-aggrandising claw-fingered scheming,

engrained inequalities and crass manipulation.
So, no, my spirits don't soar, however Romanesque
the vaults and apse, and consummate the craftsmanship:

such resource arrogation is just too grotesque.
Knock the fuckers down and build instead
decent homes for the poor sods whose strength and skills

were sequestered, for all who were cowed or misled.
Don't euphemise the raising-up of superstition and iniquity,
for however nice the architecture with its fancy historical terms
it embodies the denial by the colluding over-fed
of the people's right to fairness and prosaic dignity.

(iii) William and John

It cannot be that I'm the only one
who finds the Falstaff scenes an utter bore?
Comic relief, with bawdy, roisterous fun
the aim, I'd guess, but they scupper Henry Four.
The cackle of the crowd round hearty Jack:
the problem being, not that it's not serious,
but their blethering on about gluttony, whoring and sack
and dirty-joke punning is puerile, unfunny and tedious.
A pistol discharging, castle gates, a ruff –
why can't he stay off-stage with Hostess Quickly?
William, you're supposed to know your stuff,
but here you simply spread it on too thickly.
Relief doth not occur ere Henry Five
when good news comes: Sir John's no more alive.

Everything

The whole answer is
that there is no answer.

The whole answer is that
there is not an answer,
but bits of answers.

So much for answers;
what is there for the asking?
Same there: what we have is not a question
but bits of questions

that thin out at their own edges
and twist in and out
of the answers they fragment.

All we can do is make
a wide, slack lasso,
rope the answers and questions in,
and pen them, loosely,
where they can rub against each other
in an unanswerable
why.

Life Science

There was something in the paper
about a study where research had shown
how a fast radio burst from a dwarf galaxy
(apparently these are long-wave surges
at the far end of the electromagnetic spectrum)
emits as much energy in a millisecond
as the sun does in 10 000 years,
and then Smack!, that's it,
it's gone.

So that's where she went from here:
she seems to have bumped into
this researcher bloke,
and he's discovered what I'd already found out.

And I've also read that there are birds
that can detect infrasound disturbances
generated as storms gather beyond the horizon,
which enables them to take themselves out of harm's way
before the wind and waves arrive.

I could have done with some sensors like that.
And I'm sure that researcher bloke would agree.

One, two, three, four, five

One, two, three, four, five,
once I caught a fish alive,

six, seven, eight, nine, ten,
so did all my fellow men.

One, three, two, five, four,
not much fish left any more,

eight, seven, ten, nine, six,
think of all those factory ships.

Four, five, one, two, three,
and it is not just the sea

nine, ten, six, seven, eight,
we empty and annihilate:

five, four, three, one, two,
forest and savannah too.

Fight, ten, nine, six, seven,
everywhere our human venom.

Six, seven, eight, ten, nine,
long on poison, short on time:

five, four, three, two, one,
all our countdowns have begun.

When you're not here

I'm like a sky
without a moon
when you're away, baby;
I'm like a witch
without a broom
when you're not here.

I'm like a house
without a roof
when you're not here, baby;
I'm like a printer
with no proof
when you're away.

What good's a chimney
with no fire,
what good's a wheel
without a tyre?
What good's a door
where no-one knocks,
what good's a floor
where no-one walks?

Like an engine
with no gears
I'm sure to stall,
and like a roof
without a house
I'm sure to fall.

A horseshoe waiting for a hoof,
a theory desperate for a proof,
I'm like a bucket with no well
when you're not here, baby,
an unaimed will, not William Tell,
when you're away.
I'm like a witch
without a cat
when you're away, baby;
I'm like a witchless
witching hat
when you're not here.

A plough that's aching for a furrow,
an apple thirsting for an arrow.
What good's a wheelless wheelbarrow,
what good's today without tomorrow?

I'm like a tick
without a tock,
like them both without a clock,
I'm like a shuttle
with no loom
when you're not here, baby;
I'm like a night-sky
short of moon
when you're away.

Uptake

The way a star we see
when we see it
is not there, it's gone
since the signal was sent:

that's me –
slow on the uptake,
slow on the downbeat,
slow on the insight.

Don't think I can blame the laws of physics
for my limited vision,
limited reception:

the pulse was sent
all in cosmic good order –
be it an electromagnetic giga-surge
of urgent focused light,
particle transmission, or semaphore
(eyes, lips, fingertips);

but the force-field or entry-shield
to be overcome on approaching my atmosphere
means the source has dissolved
or simply changed co-ordinates
by the time decoding has taken place
and the signal is finally taken up.

You and Me and Leonard C

Bird on a wire?
Not me.

It's a shame and it's a pity, but
although I did my best,
I was never any good
at loving you.
You see, I was born like this,
and while your burning violin
had me kneeling at the cross of your beauty,
you closed the book of longing
and ran from love
like a refugee.

Though my promise counted for nothing,
I'll always be speaking to you sweetly
from the window of my secret life.

Moraines

Pre-millennial silt... or,
pieces which, for whatever reason,
have survived from earlier days.

Tracers

I have a wooden box
where I keep the end
of every cigarette
from the nights where I tried
to smoke you out from my room.

I have a little box
with worn-down sides
where I keep the burnt-out matches
that flickered in my fingers
in the nights where I tried
to smoke out your ghost from this room.

I have a leaden casket
where my fingers flicked the ash,
the silent ash that fell
and settled cold and grey
on the nights of trying
to smoke out your voice from my room.

I have a little window
which I open now and then
and the air comes from the mountain
to shake out the blanket
of the nights when I try
to smoke you out from my room.

You know I have a drawer
where you used to keep your things,
I keep in it three boxes
and I lean against the door
and place them every night
before me when I try
to smoke you out from my room.

Unprotected

Have you seen
beneath
the first-sight crust,

have you felt the gravity
of thirst,

been seized by the impossibility
of rest,
by the unrelenting latency
of sudden seismic burst?

Do you know
the shadow cast,
the constant receding
of every coast,
the sail the wind
has never kissed?

You get stripped down,
get pulled, get thrust,
get twisted and tripped.
You can't. You must.

You're all you've got –
you're the last you can trust.

So Many Times

So many times
I've bought a ticket, mapped out
a route, the way to go.

All the times I've upped sticks!
All those journeys on narrow tracks
with a truncated view of banks
of earth I have a feeling I recognise.

Round trip, every bloody time!

*This is a translation of my poem Så många gånger,
which was submitted as an entry in the poetry competition
run by SL, Greater Stockholm Public Transport,
and selected for inclusion in the anthology Poesi på väg
(1998, SL/Ordalaget Bokförlag, Stockholm).*

Så många gånger

Så många gånger
jag köpt biljett, klurat ut resväg, utväg.
Alla gånger jag brutit upp!
Alla dessa smalspårsresor
med utsikten kapad av vallar
av jord jag tror mig känna igen.

Tur och retur, varenda jävla gång!

Untitled

I have no title,
no nobility.
I do not register
anywhere.
The name I have –
an alias, a moniker.
I'm not entitled
to anything.

Winter light

Winter offers no escape
forces you to see
what's settled from the storm,
the minus time.

This ice pares
scalpel clean,
scrapes, delineates, renders
crystalline.

This snow
isolates, numbs,
seemingly redeemingly smoothes
all lines.

As winter collapses into spring
it forces you to see
what was beneath.
Any flowers in the grime?

You and Me

You say "I
cannot fly,
so I'll be happy on the ground."

I say "I
cannot fly,
why must I be chained down?"

You're a perfect balance
of young and old,
your spirit is strong
and your body is bold.

I'm an unsolved mix
of old and young,
years have unrolled
and nothing's got done.

A Short Song

I understand the icicles
    hanging
    from a cliff
they look like they tried
to span the divide
    but the cold made their will stiff.

It feels like the branch
    unmoving
    on the ground
stretched for light
but the weight of its life
    or the force of the storm brought it down.

I try to read the gravestones
    silent
    endless rows
collecting vats
of dripped-down wax
    the epitaphs erode.

I stand beneath the cliff
    the granite is
    austere
the touch of time
that crushes mine
    my hand leaves no mark here.

Premises

If at all
then always.

If not for ever
then never.

If not exclusively
exclude me totally,

if not with abandon
abandon me
now.

In praise of the Highland cow

The Highland cow is small and sturdy,
engaging and hirsute.
She grazes almost thoughtfully,
her strength is calm,
not brute.

I find her an uplifting sight
(what she for her part sees
is filtered through the all-round fringe
that reaches to her knees).

She's unflappable and frugal,
adaptable and tough,
her pastures may be craggy
and the weather may be rough –

none of that upsets her
unassuming age-old strain.
Against her modern breeds lack
more than upswept horns and mane.

They may be higher yielding,
those brash lab-fashioned beasts,
but their brawn is fraught with weakness:
they're too heavy for their feet;

and they're prone to pest and sickness,
and their dietary needs
demand lush grass
and vast amounts
of manufactured feed.

The small and sturdy Highland cow
is free
from their distortion;
simply
she reflects that much-neglected grace,
proportion.

In the hasp

In the hasp of these axes
the immovable graph holds sway.
We are not eternal,
I'm afraid
we're diurnal,
the night swiftly axes the day.

Concealer

You made up your face too thickly,
you made up your lies too quickly.
There was varnish on your nails
it was too thin on your tales,
it wore off and revealed your true complexion.

You talked and smiled so slickly,
but your lipstick was too sickly.
Your eyes were deep in shade
O the wounds your lashes made
when I twigged you'd shut the lid on our affection.

Composing deftly at the glass
you did not notice when I passed.
I saw your back and mirrored face
and caught a glimpse of see-through lace
that was meant for someone else's close inspection.

I noticed you'd got different clothes,
your scent was new, it stung my nose.
I put a few drops in my eyes
and your dress was such a scant disguise
it flaunted all
the shape of your deception.

Now you are with him
and grant him all
your naked skin,
but after all you masked and glossed
I'm not sure what I've really lost –
and my mirror's free to show a true reflection.

Ewig ist der Augenblick

When it comes to eternity
I take the short-term view.
The short sharp taste of time, the shock
is knocked into us, and as inexplicably withdrawn.

The only infinity
I know
is the minutes of undressing you.

Process

The thrill and glow, the founder pouring
molten metal into moulds,
metamorphic, non-conformant
supple ardent breathing gold.

Then it's finished, forged and cornered
in muted stacks it's flat and cold,
uncapricious, dense and dormant,
specified, and safe, and old.

Chronicle

Prefatory note

I'd been thinking of doing something along the lines of Louis MacNeice's Autumn Journal *for a while. During the late winter/early spring of 2016 I'd decided that the autumn of that year would be the time. This was not, however, because of any currents I had detected in the air: I had no idea what I would be writing about, or what the poem would be called or how long it would be.*

And then from June onwards, with the Brexit vote seeming to be the starting pistol, things went crazy. And it felt like there was nothing for it but to respond by starting the journal – which became Chronicle, *not* Autumn Chronicle, *since it started in June – there and then.*

I have tried to reflect various elements of MacNeice's approach; and, as he does in his prefatory note, I'd like to underline that I have not altered any content with the – benefit? blinkers? – of hindsight. So, part (ii) dates from summer 2016; part (v) from late autumn/early winter. The cut-off point is late November/early December. The view from then has not been airbrushed in the light of subsequent developments.

Lund, Sweden, early 2017

Chronicle

(i)

Close and slow, the ebb
of summer into autumn was how I thought I'd start
this chronicle, to clearly tilt my hat at Louis M.
For him the season mirrored things coming apart,
the finish of an era, of a zeitgeist, its structures dying
as the world was sucked and dragged down into war,
its end-all convulsions now large on the horizon,
now stilled into abeyance like a
collective taking-stock, a checking of the score.

Comparing the present day with 1938,
perhaps our age is more one of constant transformation
(though perhaps it's not just that change is more unleashed,
but that we feel it more, being awash with information).
Anyway,
in the respiratory rhythm of the year
autumn seemed a natural point de départ,
a time of deliberation after summer's noise and light –
though "close" and "slow" as adjectives are perhaps not really right
for the seasons here. The only slow one's winter:
slow at letting go; fast, too fast at taking hold,
muffling everything in its mantle of darkness,
snuffing out autumn, then months later
curbing spring under its clench of cold.

But so much for the idea of contemplation,
of dragging a net through the air to catch the spirit on the breeze,
steaming things into focus in the cool of the morning
with slow dark coffee as the mist sifts through the trees:

for with summer scarcely begun, with a bang and a crack
the gates of paroxysm and cataclysm blow open
as Britain spins itself into a wish to go back
to a future based in something it never was, never had.
And though unrelated, it's as if this is the starting shot
for universal fragmentation, explosion, implosion, attack:
the time is out of joint, the world
it seems is mad, nothing else than mad.
The body politic, the soul human, the very earth –
there is so much that is desperately unwell,
so much that is heavily heaped on a handcart
that is rattling straight to hell.

(ii)

Exit stage west. Semi-conscious decoupling
must now begin, for better and for worse.
The markets (whatever they are) get the jitters;
you can all but see the pounds evaporating
out of wallet and pocket and purse.
The political aftershocks begin directly,
resignations, recriminations, both sides caught on the hop.
Party splits, leadership squabbles – the rest of Europe bemused,
Britain in limbo, divided, rudders all over the shop.

And some of those who most burlesquely waved their sticks
at the rest of Europe for daring to be foreign,
and peppered the air with populist-twisted statistics,
have found there's a can to carry, having swayed the count.

And that is scary, finding out reality
is trickier than thumping tub or beating brow,

so they've shuffled off, shunning responsibility,
and you can wonder who or what they'll find to rant at now –
the price of food, taxes, the state of the NHS,
other foreign Johnnies of the non-EU persuasion,
neighbours with loud children or untrimmed hedges,
and other such signs of the crumbling of the nation.

Though I must admit that part of me is not unpleased,
for isn't one of our virtues a refusal to kow-tow?
An obstinately democratic loathness to accept
without an explanation: we want the why and how!
And yes, there's every reason for a sense of insurrection
at careerist Brusselarians with their supranational flow-charts,
in their air-conditioned, sound-proofed world of abstract non-connection
with small-scale, real-scale life. The way the Eurocrats work
is a suited, attaché-cased, lap-topped loop
of voting for themselves in a closed-circuit election.

With our spirit of dissent we give no automatic deference,
and we cherish the individual – but isn't also tolerance
a virtue we pride ourselves on, a recognition of difference?
And what about good manners? Respectful co-existence?
And I always thought that pragmatism was there among our qualities...
And come on, we're Europeans! It's one of our communities!

The nearer the referendum, the more debate lost ground
to uppity xenophobia, arms and minds began to flail,
and the self-image that stalked the land was of Richard the Crusader:
lionised, defiant, the sun shining on his mail.

And now the vote has fallen, and be everything as it may,
it's apt that in this summer of madness
an ill-mannered, intolerant, populist boor
can see his barrage win the day.

(iii)

Each of the last fourteen months the hottest ever –
it's enough to make your blood run cold.
Damned by our skewed definition of progress, of life,
where value means profits, things bought and sold,
we connive at being reduced to consumers, prisoners
to a bloodless belief that freedom of choice
means which smartphone, huge TV or olive oil.
Don't people care that they've lost their voice?
Deactivated their concern, uninstalled their connection
with life as an ongoing question, or even a quest,
a wrestling bout, with nature the mat and the rules,
where we grapple for meaning and struggle for love
and try our best to try our best.
But no, it's more important to keep updating, uploading,
spinning our web of algorithms, free as laboratory mice,
click click commissioning new reactors,
click click click melting ever more ice.

And global warming is the tip of the iceberg,
a frantic alarm screaming Fire! Wake up! Stop!
The air, the water, the soil are all in trouble!
But the money zombie does not hear, has no button for stop,
so it keeps on killing forests and overfilling the roads,
shunning balance, shunning care, investing in GMOs.
Those with power, with cash and cachet, keep on pulling the strings,
and the politicians are puppets, saying pro-puppeteer things,
and the system of abuse is kept in place with special pleading,
and everything is hurt, everything is bleeding.

(iv)

Meanwhile,
with the overall disaster as yet looming, Ragnarök
in the wings,
the world fills with eruptions that seem to symptomise
the unwellness of things;
individually, collectively, a deranged lack of perspective
and proportion spreads its black and scaly wings.

North Korea keeps on launching missiles and subs, continues
nuclear talking,
believing there's power in needling the South (and West)
with provocative squawking,
with words and deeds the vacuum-packed régime can twist when it's
its own starving people to whom it's talking.

I grew up under the leaden threat of Soviet war-heads
pointing our way.
You might think that, the cold war over, we'd allow
the dawning of a clearer day
composed of common sense and pure relief, but it can't
be ushered in with Russian belligerence blocking the way:

all those marine boundaries to flout, so much airspace
to violate,
places to annex, troops to equip and manoeuvre,
web systems to infiltrate,
dictators and mafias to back, poisons to spread: feral tsarism
sees a point of honour in nothing being inviolate.

And as if from the pressure of collective disorder
all kinds of madness break out all summer,
a miasma of must grips the world, darkens brains:
a coup and reprisals; crazed individuals
with axes, knives, guns, in shops, schools and trains.

And what about those anti-abortion extremists,
arrogating what they define as the moral stance;
all the anti-gay, anti-bi, anti-trans –
what is it that they're so afraid of?
Where does all that frightening fear begin,
fear that we see boiling into hate?
Why for them is open warmth closed off behind a gate?
Is it that inside themselves they know, without knowing
that they know, that their rigor-mortis clutch is jammed
onto something which may seem to offer them relief
from the need to question themselves, may seem positive belief,
but is in fact a pre-delineated path
based on indoctrination,
traced on someone else's words,
hemmed in by negation?

Might it be that some of these types of dislocation
are some of what's at work in the wild extremism
which more than any other blights our time, the blind tide
which can wash a man up into the cab
of a lorry which he then ploughs into the people
walking along a beach boulevard;
which means there are those who think a pure breath
inspires them to enter a church in France
and hack an old priest to death?

What underlies this unbending adherence, the rage
behind a power-crazed interpretation
of a book, and not of ideas with which one can engage?
Is it that in their zeal they're doing violence to themselves,
and by some unclear process of pressure-release
this violence must spill out and make the world its stage?

This manipulative despotism claiming to be righteous;
"If you're not with us you're against us, and then god wants you to die.
How to define against us? Easy: if you're not with us."
And when they adduce Tradition it means they close their eye
to the present and the future, and lock it on the past.
Though perhaps it's not the actual past they see,
but one which their aggressive fear wishes them to see?

Between their take and others', and within themselves,
there's this merciless divide.
How can we move all these men
to unveil their feminine side?
Prevention might have been a way – but that's no help right now.
Education for tolerance – but where is that to come from, how
can that reach through to them, and how could it influence
bombs guns machetes, macho blindness,
disrespect and hate, and know-all judge-all intransigence?

(v)

Behind the houses the tall white willows spread
their tracery against the sky. The delicate blades of green
silvered as they dried. The silver yellowed
and now the leaves, shed millions, litter
the ground. Gone the reassuring screen

whose rustling softened the grind of the motorway
that's just beyond the park.
November:
here comes the dark.

When Obama was elected it seemed to signal hope
that over there, notions like caring and justice
might still carry weight. And Michelle and Barack's warmth
underwrote those hopes,
with the love that clearly bound and bore them
informing, too, their public deeds.
But time wore on. In the land of dollar and gun
raw self-interest left ideals on the ropes,
and now, year ending, like the daylight
hope recedes.

The disbelief-beggaring presidential
campaign is over, the curtain is down.
Can you remember how, pre-nomination,
Trump was just a figure of ridicule,
a bigoted and childish clown?
He stood for selfish, unthinking materialism
and at least half the nasty isms in the book –
so no-one could possibly want him to stand for a party
as candidate for representing the country. But all it took
was a few rounds of primaries, and we could see
the punchline that was coming, could see
how the joke had turned unfunny.
This land with its partial democracy affects us all,
and when you thought about its vast reserves of inequity,
about how so many seemed sure to vote
without reference to heart or head,

thought about swing states, rust belts, and the devotion to ego and money,
all the warning signals
started flashing red.

And now the die is – the votes are – cast,
the campaign (for want of a better word) is over,
the race is run.
The closer the election came the less it seemed to matter
that he was spectacularly unfit for office:
and now he's in the oval one.

So watch it, climate.
National parks – the gauntlet has been hurled.
Take cover, social justice.
Look out, whole damn world.
We already had the blinkered global bulldozer of the yuan,
and we already had Putin in his megalomaniac bubble.
Now we've smack-it-to-'em Donald to add a spark to the mix.
We just have to hope that in the end, when all the bricks
go flying, something we can build on will survive
beneath the rubble.

    (vi)

MacNeice looked for meaning in the things we do –
or, if not in them, beneath, beyond, behind.
And he felt the need for us to believe in Life,
to live in the now in the body in the mind.
He pinned his flag to values that weigh more than fact or deed;
you might say faith in human nature,
in the strength of the committed individual
and the future of our history was his creed.

Doom was scratching at the door.
Barcelona, Munich, the final stays were being knocked out,
the total crash was being prepared: war
was shuddering into motion, a paradigm shift
that was in itself a paradigm – though beyond the horror, he felt sure,
was hope, a better, freer world to which we could lift
ourselves. And though he wondered what that day would hold,
he felt we'd get the equation right, he felt we'd pass the test.
And to break with the past he invoked restorative sleep,
and talked of creating tomorrow from a forward-looking dream.
But here, now, in this overloaded world there is no rest,
our eyes must stay wide open as we register the scene.
We live in a world where the politico-business complex
rules values, rules the rulers, numbs us with numbers.
The whole construct is overheating, boiling and leaking,
and where the hell are the plumbers?

With all we know, our science and our skills,
we could cross the Rubicon, cross the desert, cross the hills
and build beyond the formulae a life of real worth.
But is it going to happen? And is trust
in humanity and human values enough for us today?
Are we going to save the Earth?
Or are we going to throw it (scorch it,
bomb it, flood it, choke it, waste it)
throw it all away?